D1287218

GUIDES TO RESPONSIBLE HUNTING

HUNTING SAFETY, LICENSING, AND RULES

GUIDES TO RESPONSIBLE HUNTING

HUNTING ARMS

HUNTING SAFETY, LICENSING, AND RULES

PREPARING AND ENJOYING A MEAL YOU HUNTED

PREPARING FOR YOUR HUNTING TRIP

TRACKING AND HUNTING YOUR PREY

GUIDES TO RESPONSIBLE HUNTING

HUNTING SAFETY, LICENSING, AND RULES

By Elizabeth Dee

MASON CREST

Mason Crest
450 Parkway Drive, Suite D
Broomall, Pennsylvania 19008
(866) MCP-BOOK (toll-free)
www.masoncrest.com

First printing
9 8 7 6 5 4 3 2 1
Printed in the USA

ISBN (hardback) 978-1-4222-4099-1
ISBN (series) 978-1-4222-4097-7
ISBN (ebook) 978-1-4222-7698-3

Library of Congress Cataloging-in-Publication Data
Names: Dee, Elizabeth, 1957- author.
Title: Hunting safety, licensing, and rules / Elizabeth Dee.
Description: Broomall, Pennsylvania : Mason Crest, [2019] | Series: Guides for responsible hunting | Includes index.
Identifiers: LCCN 2018006639 (print) | LCCN 2018002319 (ebook) | ISBN 9781422276983 (eBook) | ISBN 9781422240991 (hardback) | ISBN 9781422240977 (series) | ISBN 9781422276983 (ebook)
Subjects: LCSH: Hunting--Safety measures. | Fish and game licenses. | Hunting--Rules.
Classification: LCC SK39.5 (print) | LCC SK39.5 .D44 2019 (ebook) | DDC 799.2028/9--dc23
LC record available at https://lccn.loc.gov/2018006639

NATIONAL HIGHLIGHTS

Developed and Produced by National Highlights Inc.
Editor: Keri De Deo
Interior and cover design: Priceless Digital Media
Production: Michelle Luke

CONTENTS

KEY ICONS TO LOOK FOR:

 Words to Understand: These words with their easy-to-understand definitions will increase the reader's understanding of the text while building vocabulary skills.

 Sidebars: This boxed material within the main text allows readers to build knowledge, gain insights, explore possibilities, and broaden their perspectives by weaving together additional information to provide realistic and holistic perspectives.

 Educational Videos: Readers can view videos by scanning our QR codes, providing them with additional educational content to supplement the text. Examples include news coverage, moments in history, speeches, iconic sports moments, and much more!

 Text-Dependent Questions: These questions send the reader back to the text for more careful attention to the evidence presented there.

 Research Projects: Readers are pointed toward areas of further inquiry connected to each chapter. Suggestions are provided for projects that encourage deeper research and analysis.

 Series Glossary of Key Terms: This back-of-the book glossary contains terminology used throughout this series. Words found here increase the reader's ability to read and comprehend higher-level books and articles in this field.

 Words to Understand:

gestation period: The length of time an animal is pregnant.

gut pile: The pile of body organs left over when field dressing an animal.

waterfowl: Birds that live and nest in marshy, wet areas such as swamps.

CHAPTER 1
PLANNING AHEAD

PLANNING AHEAD FOR YOUR HUNTING TRIP

Planning for a safe and legal hunting trip, especially if it is your first one, involves more than packing your weapon, ammunition (or ammo), and gear. Hunting game in the wild is a big step for the beginning hunter, and you'll want to do some research beforehand to help you stay safe and improve the quality of your hunting experience.

Below is a list of hunting requirements and information sources you can explore to increase your knowledge before setting off on your hunting trip.

Planning a hunting trip is more than just gathering your things.

HUNTING LICENSES AND PERMITS

You and your parents need to check into any hunting regulations and rules in your area or the location where you plan to hunt. Hunting regulations vary from each state and province, and you will need to find out the information that's correct for your specific location. If you have any questions, call or email a local game warden. You will find more information on this subject in the next chapter.

Your local game warden is an excellent resource for learning about local regulations.

HUNTING EDUCATION CERTIFICATE

Many states and provinces require that beginning hunters take classes either online or in a classroom to learn hunting safety and also to earn their Hunting Education Certificate. This certificate is a requirement for getting a hunting license. However, if beginning hunters are not old enough to get a hunting license, they are still required by many state laws to complete the training for the Hunting Education Certificate. You can study the course online. However, the final test is taken in a classroom.

Taking these classes offers a lot of educational value to the beginning hunter and helps teach some valuable hunting skills. Read more on this subject in the next chapter.

In some places, a hunting safety class is required before purchasing a license.

Since implementing the requirement of the Hunting Education Certificate with beginning hunters, the rate of hunting accidents and deaths has declined dramatically. By educating beginning hunters on the importance of gun safety and how to hunt safely and correctly, hunting has become a much safer sport that more people can enjoy.

CHECK AND REPAIR WEAPONS

To hunt safely and effectively, you need to make sure your weapons are free of rust and in good working order. Clean your firearms thoroughly and ask an adult to perform a final inspection weapon for you. Also, ask them to inspect your ammunition.

When you are hunting with a bow and arrow, hold your bow and each arrow up to a bright light and make sure there are no cracks in the material. Don't hunt with cracked bows or arrows because they can be dangerous.

If a gun or bow isn't in good working order, you will need to get it repaired by a professional. Don't try to repair a gun yourself or shoot a broken gun or arrow.

Always check your weapons for damage.

WATCH INFORMATIVE VIDEOS AND SPECIALTY TELEVISION SHOWS

There are huge amounts of information on hunting techniques and how to track birds and animals on the Internet as well as on television. You can watch videos of professional hunters showing what to pack for a trip to different climates, how to field dress a deer, how to clean a rifle, or how to use a compound bow correctly. There are also many videos about how to live off the land in case of an emergency, such as getting lost in the wilderness.

If you like to learn visually, watching educational videos is excellent for watching how something is done, such as the best way to build a campfire or skin a rabbit for cooking. Watch several videos on the same subject, such as how to clean a rifle, and see which one teaches you the most valuable information. Some instructors on the videos may be easier for you to understand. Watch several until you find the one that works best for you.

Television shows can be a valuable source of information for the beginning hunter. These shows by professional hunters can be fast paced and very interesting to watch, which makes learning fun and enjoyable.

Watching online videos can be a valuable learning tool.

READ BOOKS ON HUNTING

There are a lot of hunting classics that make great reference books for the beginning hunter and can be very entertaining to read. Books can present information in greater detail than videos or TV shows.

Check your local school library or public library to find books on hunting, tracking, or survival skills. If you can't find a book or magazine you want to read at your local library, you can request the book at the front desk. A librarian can borrow the book for you to read from another library through the interlibrary loan system. View the list of books at the back of this book for suggestions.

Your local library is a good place to find books on hunting.

PLAN YOUR PROTECTION FROM AGGRESSIVE ANIMALS AND STINGING INSECTS

Before going into the wild on a hunting trip, make sure you carry protection from wild animals, insects, reptiles, and poisonous plants. Realize the potential dangers you can be facing.

Wild animals can attack a hunter, such as packs of wild dogs, bears, or even mountain lions. You should always avoid coming face to face with these animals if possible, but if confronted by a bear, for instance, you will need some strong pepper spray to get away and not be mauled. Pepper spray causes temporary physical pain for the aggressive animal, but it will allow you to escape unhurt, and the animal won't be permanently harmed or killed.

Stinging insects that make nests in trees, in old logs, or underground are another threat to the hunter. Sometimes all it takes is for you to step on an underground nest or brush past a tree limb, and the insects will rush out and attack you. The best plan if this happens is to run away. However, if the insects get into your clothes, you can be stung multiple times. If you crush a yellow jacket, it releases a chemical that signals the others to attack. So, you should quickly brush away a yellow jacket and do not crush them. Watch out for wasp nests in low hanging tree limbs, too.

If you are allergic to any stinging insect, such a honey bee or yellow jacket, you should always carry doctor prescribed medication in your first aid kit. Tell a parent or hunting companion that you have been stung and take your medicine. You should return to camp or home immediately.

LEARN FROM MORE EXPERIENCED HUNTERS

Hands-on learning from hunters with lots of field experience can provide better results for a beginning hunter than learning from a book or video. Every successful hunter has developed their own techniques, has an expert knowledge of the animals they hunt, and have a wealth of valuable information to teach a beginning hunter. A hands-on learning experience with an expert can be the most important way to learn how to hunt if you are lucky enough to receive such instruction.

You can learn a lot from an experienced hunter.

An expert hunter knows how to handle a weapon correctly and the best way to track animals out in the wild. They respect nature and over time have developed the skills needed to stay safe and well-protected while camping and hunting. Over the years, the expert hunter taught themselves the habits of animals and birds and how to use this knowledge to their advantage when tracking small and large game.

How to Get a Hunting License

If that bare spot on your mantle is in need of a trophy buck, this video guide will get you on your way by helping you get the proper permits.

SURVIVING IN THE WILD

It's important to learn some basic survival skills.

All beginning hunters should learn some basic survival skills before going into the wilderness to hunt. If you get lost or separated from your hunting companions, you will want to know how to take care of yourself and survive long term if necessary. Learning how to recognize native plants that are edible and how to find a water source are the most important skills to know for wilderness survival.

Some adults and children have survived in the wilderness until their rescue because of skills they learned watching TV shows. However, the best way to learn survival skills is to take a hands-on course from a professional or study with an expert. Joining groups such as the Boy Scouts or Girl Scouts is also a good way to learn essential camping skills first hand and how to take care of yourself in an emergency situation if you get lost in the wild.

LEARN ABOUT THE ANIMALS OR BIRDS YOU HUNT

Learning the habits and behavior patterns of a specific animal you want to hunt makes a lot of difference in your success as a hunter. Knowing what a turkey likes to eat helps you track them by locating their food sources. Finding where a turkey gets their food helps you to discover their roosting trees where many of the birds gather.

Knowing what a turkey track looks like and the specific habitat where they like to live will help you find these elusive birds. Ducks are another bird that can be very difficult to hunt unless you know the conditions and type of locations they favor because they like to live and nest deep in marshes and swamps. Knowing how to track ducks is the only way to find these **waterfowl**.

Animal and bird activity changes with weather conditions or with the seasons of the year. For instance, deer will not venture out of their places of shelter during heavy rains or snowfalls. They also stay hidden when the weather is very hot and usually only stir from shady locations when the sun dips low on the horizon, and the air grows cooler.

Knowing a duck's habitat is important in hunting it.

Knowing when the animals give birth to their young is also an important factor for the beginning hunter to consider because you will not want to hunt during this time. Killing a mother deer, for example, means any baby fawns hidden nearby will starve to death. Shooting birds that have eggs or baby birds in their nests is another illustration of this principle. A responsible hunter will also not schedule any hunts during an animal's breeding season and **gestation period** because to do so will kill unborn babies which is unethical.

PLAN WHAT TO DO AFTER A KILL

Before you go on a hunting trip, make plans on how to process any kills. Do you want to field dress a deer yourself? Do you have the knowledge and skill to do this? Should you leave a **gut pile**? Do you want to save the head for a taxidermist to mount as a trophy? How will you store the head and the meat at a safe temperature until you reach home? Do you prefer to have the deer professionally butchered and the meat prepared? How much will such a service cost?

These are all questions you will need to answer before you go on your hunting trip. Harvesting a large animal such as

Before you go hunting, plan what you'll do with the animal afterward.

a deer can be a big responsibility and a difficult task for a beginning hunter. Smaller animals and birds aren't nearly as difficult to process and don't require as much planning.

PLAN YOUR PROTECTION FROM POISONOUS REPTILES AND PLANTS

 When it comes to poisonous snakes, the best defense is to wear good quality, snake-proof boots when hunting. You never know where in the wild you will encounter a snake, so wearing snake-proof boots when hunting means you are always protected.

Know how to recognize a poisonous snake before you go hunting. Know which snake poses a real threat to your safety and which ones are harmless; that way, you can quickly get away from a poisonous snake when you see one.

When hunting, you should always be careful when entering a place where snakes might be hiding, such as a duck blind or an enclosed deer stand. Snakes are fully capable of climbing trees, so when hunting in a forested area, be careful when walking past low hanging branches. Snakes are also attracted to water, so caution is advised when hunting in a swampy or marshy location or near lakes or streams.

If you see a snake, don't make any rapid movements and get away as quickly as you can. Snakes are usually timid creatures and try to avoid humans.

The hunter's first aid kit should always include a snakebite kit. If bitten, do not run or exert yourself in any way. Running or other physical exertion will cause the venom to spread faster through your body. Get away from the snake that bit you and quickly call for help on your cell phone. You will need to get to a hospital as soon as possible.

Poisonous plants, such as poison ivy, should also be avoided on a hunt. If you live or hunt in an area where poison ivy grows, you should know how to identify the plant before you go into the wild. Knowing what the plant looks like will help you to avoid its effects.

After a hunt in a poison ivy infested area, remove all of your clothing and wash them with hot water and strong detergent before wearing them again. Take a hot shower and scrub with a good quality soap, and wash your hair with shampoo. This procedure will not only get rid of any bad effects of poison ivy, but it will also eliminate any ticks you may have picked up in the wild.

DID YOU KNOW?

The railroad companies in the United States were directly responsible for the near extinction of the bison herds that lived on the Great Plains. The companies wanted to wipe out the gigantic herds because the bison damaged the train tracks.

When the bison herds crossed the tracks, the trains had to stop, and this interfered with the railroad's schedule. If a train couldn't stop in time and hit one or more of the bison, it caused a lot of damage to the train's engine.

As more people began to move west to take advantage of the land grants from the government, the railroad companies built more tracks and expanded their transportation lines. These companies saw the American bison as a threat to their enterprise and wanted the herds completely eradicated from the Great Plains and totally exterminated.

Bison were nearly hunted to extinction.

The railroad companies hired professional game hunters to travel to the Great Plains and kill as many bison as possible. Trains packed with hunters would ride up and down the railroad lines, and the men would shoot the bison from the windows.

Railroad workers would come behind the trains and drag the carcasses away to process for meat, hides, and bones. The meat was cooked and eaten by the railroad employees, the hides were made into rugs, coats, or sold abroad, and farmers ground the bones into a cheap fertilizer.

Some professional game hunters would ride out on horseback, kill the bison, and leave the carcass untouched. The Native American tribes of the area began to complain of this mass slaughter and waste of valuable resources. The tribes depended upon the herds of bison for a major source of food. However, the powerful railroad companies saw the elimination of the bison as a step toward getting rid of the Native American tribes as well.

The plan to exterminate the bison herds and replace them with herds of cattle had a disastrous effect on the ecosystem of the Great Plains. Modern experts believe problems began because the bison was well adapted to survive on the Great Plains, and cattle are not so well suited.

Cattle eat away the native grass, but not tree sprouts like the bison. This process allows trees to grow and take over, which eventually kills other vegetation and endangers the grasslands of the prairie. Cattle damage has also caused a lot of soil erosion in the area. Also, cattle need a lot more water to survive than bison, and this has put a strain on natural water resources as well. Bison are considered to be much more environmentally friendly than other livestock.

Do you know the difference between a buffalo and a bison? When the first settlers, originally from other countries, began to move west into the Great Plains to stake claims for homesteads, they marveled at the great herds of these gigantic animals that lived on the prairie. The settlers thought these huge creatures looked a lot like the Asian water buffalo, so they began mistakenly calling the bison a "buffalo."

An Asian water buffalo is different from a bison.

TEXT-DEPENDENT QUESTIONS:

1. Why should you learn as much as possible about the animals or birds you want to hunt?

2. Why is it best to learn hunting skills from an expert hunter?

3. How do you avoid getting snake bit in the wild?

RESEARCH PROJECT:

Make a detailed list of every item you need to take on a single day, local hunting trip. Show this list to at least two more experienced hunters. What is their opinion of the items you have chosen? Do they think you omitted anything important? What are their reasons for thinking this?

Write a two-page paper about your hunting list and the other hunters' opinions on your choice of items. Discuss the things you forgot to add and why the other hunters' thought those items were necessary to take on the hunt. Write about the items you chose that were correct as well.

Show the paper to several of your friends who are also hunters. What are their opinions? Do they have anything to add to your list?

Write the more experienced hunters' opinions, as well as your friends' ideas, in your hunting journal if you keep one.

 Words to Understand:

deer cooler: A business that commercially processes deer for the venison.

permit: A statement of legal permission from the government to hunt in your location.

poaching: Killing an animal or bird illegally for profit. Some poachers kill endangered animals and sell their body parts online.

youth hunter: The term used to describe a young hunter by governmental institutions.

THE PURPOSE OF HUNTING REGULATIONS

Hunting rules and regulations exist for the protection of the hunter as well as the conservation and maintenance of wildlife. Different institutions govern the hunting activities of each U.S. state and Canadian province.

Each state and province also has a different set of regulations for hunting and fishing in that location. To find out the specific hunting regulations for your particular area, you need to visit your local government's website.

Some hunting rules vary depending on the state or province.

WHAT YOU NEED LEGALLY

Beginning hunters under the age of twelve rarely need a hunting license. However, the regulations state that **youth hunters** must be in the company of a fully licensed adult at all times during a hunt. They are not allowed to hunt alone. Youth hunters are usually allowed to apply for their own hunting license when they reach the age of sixteen. Some states offer a reduced rate for teen hunters.

If you want to take a trip and go hunting in another state, an adult will need to purchase a separate hunting license that's valid in that state for the two of you to legally hunt in that location. Non-resident hunting licenses are typically more expensive than one bought in one's home state.

Most state and provinces require a hunting license.

Hunters born after the year 1949 now require a Hunter Education Certificate that shows they have taken the required educational courses on hunting safety, gun handling, and other subjects to get a valid hunting license in their state.

Some state governments encourage hunters to apply and renew their hunting licenses online, claiming there are fewer mistakes on the applications. States such as Colorado have decided to go paperless and process all hunting licenses on their website.

YOU MAY NEED A TAG

You may also need a tag to hunt larger game animals. Tags are extra **permits** you need to legally hunt animals such as deer, moose, elk, wild boar, or bears. Typically, a hunter receives a limited number of tags per hunting season. The hunter is allowed to kill one animal per tag.

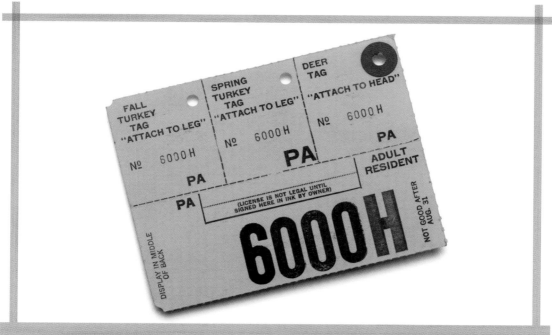

A hunting tag is often required.

When an animal is shot and killed, a deer, for example, the hunter is required by law to fill the tag out and then attach it to the deer. The information to be written on the tag includes such facts as the time and date of the kill, the approximate location, and a general description of the deer. For example, you would write a "six-point buck" on the tag as your description.

A hunter should always carry the tags in a pocket for easy access during a hunt. If a game warden catches a hunter with a fresh kill and no tag, they will be in violation of the law. The hunter will have to pay a fine, have their hunting license revoked, or both.

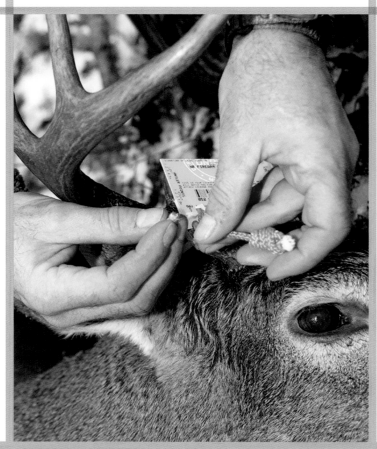

A fresh kill must be tagged for it to be legal.

WHAT IS A GAME WARDEN?

 Game wardens are known by many different names depending on where in the USA or Canada you live. Wildlife officer, fish and game officer, and conservation officer are three of the most common names or titles. Game wardens are employed by the state government to prevent illegal poaching and otherwise protect the state's fish and wildlife. These public officials are very much like the police in that they patrol parks and other public lands watching out for hunting and fishing violations by individuals or businesses. They also patrol remote areas, mountains, rivers, and lakes looking for any signs of illegal hunting.

These officials are very active during hunting seasons, making sure hunters tag their kills and only harvest as many animals as allowed per person. They also check to make sure hunters or fishermen are carrying valid and up-to-date licenses.

Game wardens make sure that environmental laws are upheld to protect wildlife from industrial pollution such as waste products from manufacturing plants. These officials work hard to prevent the illegal poaching of endangered animals and birds, as well as the destruction of their habitats. They also are trained in first aid and routinely rescue people that are stranded, lost, or hurt in the wild.

Some game wardens are killed in the line of duty. Working to protect the environment from unlawful hunting and poaching and preventing illegal trade of birds or animals can be a dangerous job.

OTHER HUNTING REGULATIONS

ARCHERY

Some states will only allow bow hunting for deer in certain counties and at specific times in what is called "primitive weapon seasons." Hunters are not allowed to hunt with any firearm during this time, only bows and arrows. However, during primitive weapon season, you can hunt deer with a gun if you are under sixteen years of age.

Bow hunting comes with its own rules and regulations.

THE SIZE OF AN ANIMAL'S ANTLERS MATTER

Some states have restrictions concerning the size of a deer's antlers at certain times of the year. The antler spread must be of a small size before a youth hunter can hunt the animal. This law is to prevent injuries to a youth hunter by an animal with large and dangerous antlers. This same law applies to caribou, elk, and moose.

Deer that have no antlers may only be hunted during special antlerless hunts or during a season where deer of both sexes may be hunted. If the state proclaims a buck-only hunt, you cannot hunt the males that have no antlers or only very small antlers.

Some states restrict youth hunters from hunting animals with large antlers.

REMOVING AN ANIMAL'S HEAD

Some states have laws regarding the removal of a large game animal's head, such as a deer, for mounting as a trophy. Some states will not allow the removal of the head of a deer until the animal has been taken to a processing facility.

Check the local laws before removing the head from a harvested animal.

LOCATION IS IMPORTANT

Some states will not allow a hunter to kill a deer when it is by a body of water, such as a lake or stream.

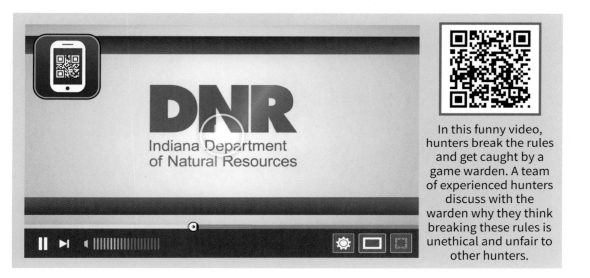

In this funny video, hunters break the rules and get caught by a game warden. A team of experienced hunters discuss with the warden why they think breaking these rules is unethical and unfair to other hunters.

WEARING BLAZE ORANGE OR HUNTER'S ORANGE

It is a requirement in some states and provinces that all hunters wear a bright, fluorescent orange color called blaze orange during deer season. This color stands out against the surrounding landscape making the hunter highly visible to other hunters in the area. Blaze orange protects hunters from being accidentally shot while hunting with others. Some states also require hunters to wear this color during hunts for wild boar and bears.

Some states, such as Virginia, also allow hunters to wear a bright, fluorescent pink color, called blaze pink. This color is a favorite of many female hunters.

Some birds, such as turkeys, can see blaze orange. However, deer, wild boars, and bears can't see the color.

Most states require that you wear blaze orange for safety.

Hunters should wear blaze orange for their protection. Some states, such as Alaska or California, don't legally require anyone to wear the color, but they do encourage hunters to wear it for their safety. Other states have requirements that a certain amount of blaze orange is worn. Check on the Internet to see the requirements of your specific state or province.

USE YOUR PHONE OR COMPUTER

Some states offer cell phone apps where you can enter the kill date, time, and location while still in the field or before you take your harvest to be processed at a **deer cooler**. When using the app to report your kill, you will be given a confirmation number. This app makes it easier to report and keep a record.

You can also use your computer to visit a website or call a phone number listed on the site to record your kill. The time limit to do this is usually 72 hours.

TRUST YOUR INTUITION WHILE HUNTING

 So many times, in the past, veteran hunters have said, "I had a feeling not to shoot," when discussing a particular incident. Or they would say, "Something told me not to shoot, and I'm glad I didn't." That mysterious "something" that warned them not to shoot was their natural intuition, and in all the cases the hunters later said they were very glad they paid attention to those feelings.

Sam Carreker, a seasoned hunter, relied on his feelings or intuition many times during his long career as a hunter and as a result, he never was involved in a serious accident. One year, when a very large fox was raiding the local hen houses and killing a lot of poultry, the farmers asked Sam and some of his hunter friends to do something about it. A couple of farmers stated they had spotted a large fox in a wooded area nearby.

The hunters set out one sunny day with their hunting dogs. Fanning out in a large wooded area, my dad and his hunting companions roamed through the woods with the dogs, hunting for that elusive fox.

Sam passed through a clearing on the crest of a hill when he heard the dogs baying in the distance and a lot of rustling in the bushes in front of him. Sam was excited. He knew it must be the fox running from the dogs. He stopped, raised his rifle to his shoulder, and waited. The rustling grew closer. Something was coming up the hill at a very rapid and noisy pace. That's when he had a "feeling" to put down the gun.

He lowered his rifle. Suddenly, a dog popped over the crest of that ridge and right behind the dog was Sam's hunting friend. This incident happened years before hunters began wearing blaze orange as protection, so the other hunter was difficult to see. My dad's intuition prevented a potentially fatal accident.

Lots of hunters talk about using their "feelings" when tracking animals. How they "just know" when a rabbit or deer will be in a certain spot. This is an example of human's natural intuition or instinct. Learn to pay attention to such feelings, and they will help you be a better hunter.

DID YOU KNOW?

William Frederick Cody, best known by his nickname of Buffalo Bill, was a famous hunter and showman of the American Old West. Bill rode horses constantly and became a master horseman. As a child of fourteen, he worked for the Pony Express, delivering messages for wagon teams to make money to support his mother after his father died. Bill also worked as an Army scout and a professional hunter. Hunting bison for the Kansas Pacific Railroad is how he earned his make Buffalo Bill.

Buffalo Bill's favorite gun was a Springfield Model 1866 service rifle which was a common gun of the time. The breech-loaded weapon was a standard issue to United States Army soldiers and was famous for its rapid fire of ammunition. Bill named his rifle Lucretia Borgia, after the notorious woman poisoner.

In 1893, Buffalo Bill started his own Wild West show which was a popular form of entertainment of the time. Wild West Shows featured lots of loud music and actors that did fantastic rope tricks, cowboys that performed dangerous stunts with livestock or wild animals, and men and women who held shooting exhibitions that shocked and amazed the crowds. Native American performers dressed in their tribal clothes were also very popular. Wild West Shows were very popular in urban areas of the United States and other countries where people were fascinated by the romanticized version of the Wild West.

Buffalo Bill was a very handsome man and his appearance helped draw crowds of spectators to his show. He became so popular that he traveled with his Wild West show to England where he performed for Queen Victoria and other heads of state, such as the Prince of Wales. Kaiser Wilhelm II also attended the show and was very impressed!

Buffalo Bill was a famous hunter and showman in the 1800s.

TEXT-DEPENDENT QUESTIONS:

1. What is a tag used for when hunting?

2. What is a game warden, and what function do they serve?

3. Why should you wear blaze orange while hunting?

RESEARCH PROJECT:

For this project, you can either use a large poster or individual sheets of paper. Do an online search of the hunting regulations for all the states if you live in the United States and all the provinces if you live in Canada. You can either draw a chart on the poster board or use individual sheets of paper for each state or province to map out the different laws.

Compare the different laws of each state or province. How do the regulations and laws differ from region to region? How are they alike? Do you detect any similarities? What do you think is the reasoning behind each law?

Write a three-page paper on your findings and present it to three adult hunters and also to some of your friends who are interested in hunting. What are their opinions on these laws and regulations? Do they believe the laws are necessary or should some of the regulations be changed?

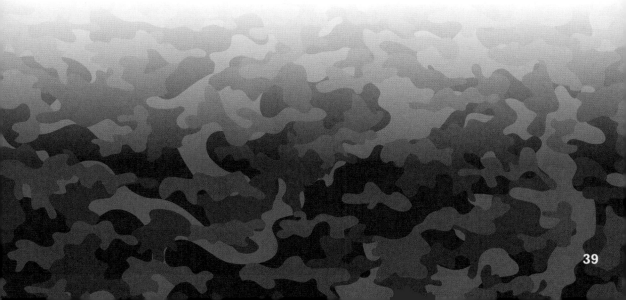

 Words to Understand:

bone-free: Butchered meat that has the bones taken out if it.

Chronic Wasting Disease: A terminal sickness that kills antlered animals, such as deer, by slowly destroying their brains.

taxidermist: A person who preserves the bodies of animals, fish, or birds as hunting trophies.

REGULATIONS CONCERNING DIFFERENT GAME TYPES

For the different types of animals, there are separate sets of regulations. For deer, pronghorn, elk, moose, and caribou, laws have been put in place to help deal with **Chronic Wasting Disease**.

Rules for hunting large game, like caribou, vary from small game because of CWD.

LAWS REGARDING CHRONIC WASTING DISEASE

One main concern of wildlife management is the growing threat of Chronic Wasting Disease. Laws have been passed regarding the meat of animals sick with Chronic Wasting Disease, or CWD, a serious and fatal neurological illness that mainly affects caribou, elk, moose, pronghorn, white-tailed deer, mule deer, and Coues deer. Over the past years, CWD has continued to spread through the United States and into Canada.

If you hunt in a state or province where CWD has been confirmed in animal herds, you are only allowed to bring back certain parts of your kill to your home.

In areas where CWD has been detected, you are only allowed to bring home certain parts of the animal.

This harvest list is what most regulations allow hunters to bring across state lines:

- Antlers that have been thoroughly cleaned.
- The part of the skull with the antlers. You can't bring the whole skull.
- Animal heads processed by a professional **taxidermist**.
- Meat that has been processed and is **bone-free**.

The reason for these regulations is to prevent the spread of CWD to other states. CWD is a major threat to the health of many large game animals all around the world, and government officials are working hard to keep this sickness from spreading. You can't usually tell if an animal is sick with CWD unless it is in the last stages of the illness. Then the animal appears very thin and looks sick.

If an animal you harvest looks sick, leave it and contact the nearest game warden. It could have CWD.

If you kill an animal and it looks sick, you should not butcher or field dress the body. Just leave the carcass where it fell and ask an adult to report the location of the sick animal to the nearest game warden. You should not under any circumstances eat the meat of a sick-looking animal. Some states require that animals killed in that state need to be tested for CWD before they can be processed.

Before going hunting, you should check the regulations concerning Chronic Wasting Disease in your state. Are the deer, elk, or caribou herds in your area affected by CWD? To be on the safe side, don't take any chances when handling a deer carcass. Discuss this topic with your parents and any other adult that is your hunting companion.

BE EXTRA CAREFUL OF RABIES

You should always be careful of rabies when hunting. Large animals, such as deer, as well as small warm-blooded mammals, such as rabbits, can become infected with this deadly disease. If you see an animal, such as a deer, with a staggering gait, foaming at the mouth, or acting in an unusually aggressive manner, you should get away from that animal quickly and contact a game warden to investigate the situation. If you do shoot the animal before realizing it has rabies, be sure not to touch the carcass and ask an adult to contact a game warden as quickly as possible.

If you accidentally come in contact with a rabid animal while hunting and are bitten or scratched, you must report this to your parent or a responsible adult and see a doctor immediately. Rabies spreads quickly and is always fatal to humans and animals if not treated as soon as possible. You must get medical attention as quickly as you can.

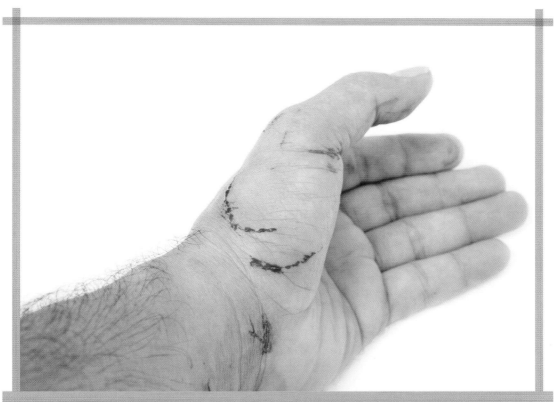

To stay safe from rabies, quickly report any bite or scratch from a wild animal.

HUNTING SHOULD NOT BE A COMPETITIVE SPORT

 When hunting with others, it's easy to become competitive with your friends, to keep score, and try to outdo the others. However, being competitive while hunting is a very dangerous thing to do. It can cause you to become reckless and have an accident.

Don't ever bet a friend that you can kill more squirrels than they can, or more turkeys, or deer. A little friendly competition while target practicing on a range is fine but never out in the wild when hunting living creatures. Hunting in the wild should never involve any competition. If you are competing with someone during a hunt, you will not focus as much on safety.

YOUTH HUNTERS AND ANTLERLESS WILD GAME

Some states, such as Colorado, have laws that govern what kind of wildlife youth hunters are allowed to hunt. Youth hunters between the ages of twelve and seventeen are not allowed to hunt deer, elk, or other horned animals that have large antler growth that could be dangerous to a human. They can only hunt a deer, for example, that has no antlers or very small antlers. This means either a young male or a doe. Youth hunters also need a special type of license that specifies they can only hunt antlerless game.

Some states limit what youth hunters can hunt.

In past years, some states limited youth hunters to only hunting late in the season. However, this is changing, and youth hunters are allowed to hunt for a longer period of time during some hunting seasons. Youth hunters are also given tags to fill out if they make a kill.

Youth hunters can hunt antlerless game, such as young bucks, with firearms as well as with bows and arrows. However, some states restrict the dates and locations for the use of hunting bows. Youth hunters can also be restricted to certain areas when they hunt. Sometimes they will not be allowed to hunt in locations with dangerous terrain.

When hunting with a bow, it is illegal to carry a firearm and ammunition. You should only have a bow and arrows with you.

Youth hunters are required by law not to hunt big game alone and should always be accompanied by an adult with a valid hunting license. One adult can supervise only one youth hunter and not a group of youths in some states, while others will allow one adult for two youth hunters. Check your specific state or province to find out the laws in your location.

In some locations, young hunters are required to be accompanied by an adult.

Cooking Wild Game: Venison Marsala.

TURKEY HUNTING FOR YOUTHS

Check the regulations about youth hunters in your area.

The regulations for age limits drop when it comes to hunting turkeys. Some states allow youth hunters as young as five years old to hunt turkeys when accompanied by a fully licensed adult. However, the time allowed for the hunt is very short. Youth hunters are only allowed to hunt turkeys for thirty minutes per day and during daylight hours.

When it comes to hunting turkeys, game wardens frown on the use of electronic devices that imitate the call of the birds, night vision devices, or a living decoy. However, most states permit the youth hunter to hunt turkeys with bows and arrows.

Hunting regulations only allow youth hunters to kill a certain number of these birds and sometimes only male turkeys can be hunted. Sometimes the harvest number for the spring hunting season is as low as one turkey per season. Later in the year, during the fall season, this number can rise to two turkeys. These harvest numbers remain the same whether you are hunting with a firearm or a bow.

BE CAREFUL WITH YOUR HUNTING TAGS

When hunting turkeys, government officials recommend that youth hunters carry paper hunting tags in their pockets in a plastic, see-through bag and attach the tag to the turkey's leg for easy identification for a game warden. Don't punch a hole or notch the paper until you have harvested an animal or bird because doing so without a kill will make the tag invalid.

Don't play around with your paper tag or lose it! Keep the paper safe and dry in a plastic bag and keep it secure in the deep pocket of your hunting jacket. You don't want to lose the opportunity to harvest a turkey because of carelessness. If you harvest a turkey, you don't want to lose the tag afterward and get into trouble. If you need help, ask a parent or another adult to keep the tag safe for you.

HUNTING GOOD SENSE

If you want to hunt on private land, always ask a parent or adult to obtain permission to hunt from the owner first. When hunting, don't cross any boundaries onto private land without permission. If you are chasing a deer, for instance, and the animal crosses onto private land, do not follow.

When hunting on private land, be sure not to leave any litter, such a food wrappers or soda bottles or cans. Make sure to pick up all empty ammunition cartridges and locate all your arrows. If an arrow is not retrievable, then ask your parent to tell the landowner what happened. Always hunt with an adult on private land and never alone.

If you do not kill an animal or bird when you first shoot it, you should get an adult to assist you with killing the creature swiftly so it will not continue to suffer. Don't play games with a wounded animal or try to tease it in any way. Be respectful of all wildlife and merciful to the wounded.

Respect the property of others and obey all signs.

DID YOU KNOW?

Poaching has always been an illegal activity all over the world and throughout history. In the Medieval Ages, it was a crime that was often punished by death or dismemberment. Sometimes the poacher would have their hands or an arm cut off if they were found guilty of stealing wild game animals and birds from the aristocrats that owned the land.

Peasants that poached game usually did so with a simple trap or snare. Poachers of that time usually stole the wild game because of crop failure, and their families were starving. The severe punishment for poaching kept most peasants from unlawfully trapping game unless they were desperate.

By the 18th century, poaching was a way of life for some individuals in Europe. They trapped game to stay alive because of climate changes that caused harsh winters and shorter growing seasons for crops. Food became scarce in many areas, and poachers turned to the local wildlife to feed themselves and their families.

In this century, poachers in the United States and Canada kill big game animals such as big horned sheep, bears, moose, elk, and deer. They also poach smaller animals, such as mountain goats, and birds, such as turkeys and pheasants. It's a game warden's job to try and stop these illegal hunters from poaching game.

All over the world, various animals are killed illegally for their body parts. Tigers are trapped and killed for many reasons. Their bones are ground and made into wine, the striped skins are used to manufacture decorative items, and other parts, such as the blood and eyes, are used to make medicine in Asia.

Gangs of nomads in India hunt the tigers with big steel traps that are made in secret. The gangs set out the traps on nights when the moon is bright, so they don't have to use flashlights and risk being caught. Since they do not live in one place, these gangs will hunt in an area and move on before the authorities realize what is happening. Once a tiger is caught, the gang will kill and strip

Tigers are often poached for their body parts and not for food.

the tiger of the skin and other body parts in just a few hours. Poachers sell these items on the black market for high prices.

Elephants have long been victims of illegal poaching through the years and their tusks sold on the black market. Ivory from the tusks is used primarily in China to make luxury items. Up until the 1980s, piano keys were made out of ivory.

TEXT-DEPENDENT QUESTIONS:

1. What deer parts are you allowed to bring across state lines because of CWD?

2. What do you do if you suspect a wild animal has rabies?

3. How do you keep a paper hunting tag safe while hunting?

RESEARCH PROJECT:

Research how many cases of rabies have been documented in your state over the last twelve months. How many people were infected? Were there any fatalities? Talk with at least three experienced hunters and ask if they have had any experience with a rabid animal. Were they scratched or bitten?

Write a four-page paper on the effects of rabies on the body of humans as well as animals. Present your paper to your class, friends, and family. What are their reactions? Did they know that rabies was such a deadly disease?

 Words to Understand:

blind: A small shelter built in the wild for hunters to observe wildlife.

etiquette: The rules of good manners and behavior.

CHAPTER 4
HUNTING ETIQUETTE (UNSPOKEN RULES)

THE HUNTER'S CODE OF HONOR

The sport of hunting has a code of ethics. Governmental institutions consider some practices acceptable and some unlawful and destructive to the environment and other hunters. It is up to every individual hunter to follow a code of honor and have respect for hunting laws and regulations.

HUNTING ON FARMLAND

If you are allowed to hunt on a farm, please be respectful. Be careful when crossing a field not to destroy any crops or disturb the soil in any way. If you have a driver's license, don't drive a vehicle across a field, whether crops are growing in it or not. Farm fields have soft, plowed dirt good for growing fruits and vegetables, and if you drive over the area, you will compact the soil. Compacted soil will have to be plowed again to loosen the dirt. Don't create unnecessary work for the farmer.

When crossing open pastures, be careful not to disturb any livestock. Bulls and other male animals such as goats can be aggressive and unpredictable to a young hunter. If a bull with large, sharp horns is in a pasture, you should probably not cross the area. It's better to walk further around the pasture than be attacked by the bull. Very young animals, too, can be frightened by loud sounds, such as gunshots.

If you need to pass through a closed gate, please be sure to close it behind you. If there is a latch, be sure to latch the gate behind you. By not closing or latching a gate, any livestock in the pasture can escape, and it will take a farmer a long time to round up all the animals again.

Always ask permission before hunting on farmland,
and be respectful of the property.

Escaped livestock can do a lot of damage to other people's property, such as eat expensive landscaping plants or a field of vegetables. The animals can also wander onto a road and be hit by a passing vehicle. For all of this, the farmer who owns the livestock will be legally liable. You don't want to get the farmer in trouble after he kindly allowed you to hunt on his farm!

DON'T LEAVE BEHIND ANY TRACES YOU HUNTED THERE

Whether you are hunting on private or public land, don't disturb the landscape. If you are putting up a tree stand on private land, only do so after your parent has asked permission from the landowner. Don't cut down any trees, cut off branches, chop down any bushes or shrubs, or trample down tall grass. You want to leave the location exactly like you found it.

Pick up your gun shells, and leave no trace that you were there.

If you plan to camp on someone's land and want to have a campfire, you should make sure a parent asks permission first. Before making the campfire, you will need to dig a pit and line the rim with rocks to keep the fire contained. It's a good idea to keep a container filled with water nearby to pour over the fire and extinguish any live coals before you leave the area. When you are ready to leave the campsite, douse the fire with water, especially if the weather has been dry.

Make sure you pick up all trash and food scraps around your camp after eating. If you need to have a bowel movement, dig a small, deep hole for the purpose, and cover it up when finished. If you butcher or field dress an animal or bird, you should show respect to the landowner by either burying the gut pile (with permission) or taking away the complete carcass.

If you find litter on someone's land left behind by hunters, such as empty shell cases, be considerate and pick up the cases and dispose of them.

If you find trash that someone else left behind, don't leave it there.

BE AS QUIET AS POSSIBLE

When hunting on private or public land, you should be considerate of other hunters and make as little noise as possible. Don't shout or yell back and forth with your other hunting buddies, talk in a loud voice, or do anything that would make a lot of noise and ruin the hunting for other hunters in the area. Avoid running through underbrush or dry leaves.

You also need to make sure your hunting gear doesn't rattle or make other sounds as you walk. Animals, such as deer or elk, have very keen hearing, and sometimes the slightest sound will scare them enough to run. If you are old enough to drive, remember not to honk car or truck horns near a hunting area.

If you are walking through the woods or open field and happen to pass another hunter, let the person know you are there, but try to make as little noise as you can manage. The hunter may be watching a bird or animal and waiting for an opportunity to take a shot. You don't want to ruin the other hunter's chances.

Be careful not to disturb other hunters by being too loud.

HAVE A BACKUP PLAN

 You wake up early one Saturday morning before dawn excited about the hunting trip you and your dad have planned for weeks. You quickly dive into your clothes, eat breakfast, and grab your backpack of carefully packed hunting gear.

You and your dad arrive at your favorite hunting spot only to find another hunter already there. They've even put in a portable tree stand in "your" tree! What do you do?

This is public land, so the other hunter has just as much right to hunt in your favorite spot as you do. You will need to find another hunting place for that day.

When planning a hunting trip, it's best to have a backup plan of several locations where you can hunt. Make a list of possible hunting places beforehand and mark several areas on a map. That way, if someone else takes that spot before you do, you can just go to the next one on your list.

Some hunters can get irritated if they find someone else in their favorite location. If another hunter approaches you or your hunting companions with an angry attitude and says you are in their hunting spot, just leave. It's best not to argue with anyone. Just move on to another place. Who knows, you may have some phenomenal luck there!

DON'T TRESPASS

When hunting, you need to be extra careful when it comes to the boundaries of public land and private land. You should always have a clear idea of the location of these boundaries while on a hunting trip. Sometimes landowners put up trespass warning signs along the edges of their property, indicating the area is privately owned land, and this can help guide you. Never go onto private land without getting the owner's permission first.

Don't let a hunting friend convince you that it's okay to hunt on private land without permission. Don't hunt on private land without an adult.

Get permission before hunting on private property.

A landowner needs to know if other people are using firearms or archery on his property, so he can take precautions, such as keeping small children or pets indoors until the hunt is over. It's not only good hunting **etiquette** to ask a landowner's permission; it's a safety issue as well.

Don't shoot near a landowner's house or any outbuildings such as barns or chicken houses and be careful not to shoot in that direction while hunting. Never shoot in the direction of children's swing sets, playhouses, vehicles, RVs, or popup campers that may be parked on the property.

This video gives a lot of practical advice for choosing a hunting spot on public land.

RESPECT ANOTHER'S PROPERTY

If you hunt on your land or with a hunt club, and you and your family have built a permanent tree stand or a **blind** that you regularly use during hunting season, make sure your name or your family's name is clearly marked on the stand or the blind. That way another hunter will know who the stand or blind belongs to and will not be tempted to use it.

If you see a permanent tree stand or a blind that is unmarked, don't be tempted to use it without the owner's permission. The tree stand or blind belongs to someone, and you should respect their property.

BE CONSIDERATE CONCERNING GUT PILES

When field dressing an animal, be considerate of other people and don't dump the gut pile, hides, or bones near public places, such as beside the road or near a commercial area or parking lot. You don't want to turn other people against the sport of hunting by causing a disgusting mess.

Don't leave behind a gut pile without checking regulations.

Not only will other people have to endure the smell as the gut pile and other body parts decompose, but it can draw scavenger animals or birds to the area where they can get run over by passing cars or trucks or possibly try to bite a person or pet.

Another reason a hunter should never leave gut piles in areas with a lot of traffic is Chronic Wasting Disease. Many deer now live in suburban areas and could be infected by a gut pile taken from a sick animal and left out in the open.

COVER YOUR KILL WHEN IN PUBLIC

Some wildlife associations and hunters believe you should never display your animal or bird harvests in public because some non-hunters are very sensitive to the fact that an animal has been killed. The unwelcome sight of a dead animal can also frighten or upset small children. Traveling down the highway with a dead deer in the back of a truck may attract some unwelcome and unfriendly attention, plus it is very disrespectful to the deer. You or your family or hunting friends don't want to appear to others to be a show-off.

Cover a large animal, such as a deer or elk, if you are transporting it in the back of a pickup truck without a camper top. Use a large tarp and rope to secure the tarp and keep it from blowing off the animal and out of the back of the truck. Don't brag about your hunting harvests to other people who may not understand the ethics of hunting.

BE CONSIDERATE OF NATURE

You don't need to shoot a lot of animals or birds to have a fun time hunting. Learn to enjoy the whole experience of getting out in nature and watching the wildlife. Learn the exciting sport of how to handle and shoot a gun or bow. Learn the amazing skill of how to survive in the wilderness. Most of all, don't kill just for the sheer sport of killing. To kill and waste the meat is not what the sport of hunting represents. Humans need to support the ecosystem of the earth, so that Earth, in turn, can continue to support humankind.

A good hunter cares deeply about conserving nature and preserving the wilderness for future generations. They know that herds of deer need to be thinned out periodically, for example, for the health of the herd and the whole ecosystem. A good hunter is not ashamed of hunting for meat to feed themselves and their families as long as they respect and follow the hunter's code of honor.

You don't have to have a successful kill to enjoy a trip in the forest.

Be considerate, and cover your kill when in public.

DID YOU KNOW?

The most valuable hunting dog throughout history is the swift and elegant greyhound. No other breed of dog can run faster and catch prey quicker than these graceful, beautiful dogs, which have been known to reach speeds of over 40 mph (64 kmph). Not only can greyhounds be trained into highly-skilled hunters, but they are also extremely gentle by nature and are unusually devoted to their owners.

Throughout history, a greyhound was called a "sighthound" because of their excellent ability to spot prey at a distance. Due to these dogs' fast speeds and large sizes, a greyhound is capable of bringing down large prey, and for centuries they were prized as the best hunters throughout history. It was only in the last 100 years that greyhounds were used as racing animals after hunting became a less popular sport.

Greyhounds were once used as hunting dogs.

The greyhound was so valued throughout history that they became the favorite dogs of kings, emperors, and even pharaohs. Greyhounds are featured as fierce hunting dogs in Egyptian hieroglyphs, and their bodies were mummified and buried in tombs with their royal masters. Even the Egyptian god Anubis has the head of a greyhound.

All through the centuries, rulers and their royal families so loved the greyhound that ordinary people were not allowed to own these dogs. Even in Ancient Egypt, killing a greyhound was considered such a terrible crime that it carried a death sentence for the person.

Queen Victoria and her husband, Prince Albert, owned many dogs, but a black and white greyhound named Eos, after the Greek goddess of the dawn, was the favorite! Eos was a fierce hunter, but so gentle and loving to her human family that a famous artist painted her with her head lying sweetly on the feet of the royal couple's baby.

Queen Victoria's uncle, Prince Ferdinand, accidentally shot Eos while on a hunt. Prince Albert ordered that his favorite pet receive the best of care. Eos lived on, and she eventually died of old age in 1844. Prince Albert, who had raised Eos from a little puppy, was heartbroken. The much-loved greyhound was buried on the grounds of Windsor Castle. A bronze statue of Eos stands at Osborne House.

The bronze statue of the greyhound Eos still stands at the Osborne House.

TEXT-DEPENDENT QUESTIONS:

1. Why should a hunter not talk loudly during a hunt?

2. Why should you have a backup plan of several different locations before going on a hunting trip?

3. What are two reasons a landowner should know if someone is hunting on their property?

RESEARCH PROJECT:

For this project, you will need a copy of your state or province hunting regulations. You can find these on the Internet.

Make a list of twenty hunting regulations. Why do you think each regulation is needed to protect wildlife and the public? Research and find out as much information as possible about each of the twenty regulations. Write about the differences of your thoughts and the information you find in your research.

Using the twenty hunting regulations of your state or province, write a three-page paper on your findings. Show your report to three experienced hunters and ask their opinion of the twenty hunting regulations. Do their opinions differ from yours?

Briars: A patch of thick underbrush that is full of thorny bushes. Rabbits and other small game love to hide in these.

Burrow: A hole made by a small animal where they live and stay safe from predators. It is also the word for what an animal does when it digs these holes.

Carcass: The dead body of an animal after the innards have been removed and before it has been skinned.

Field dress: To remove the inner organs from an animal after it has been harvested. It's important to field dress an animal as quickly as possible after it has been harvested.

Habitat: The area in which an animal lives. It's important to preserve animal habitats.

Hide: The skin of an animal once it has been removed from the animal. Hides can be made into clothing and other useful gear.

Homestead: A place or plot of land where a family makes their home. This is different from habitat because it is manmade.

Kmph: An abbreviation for kilometers per hour, which is a metric unit of measurement for speed. One kilometer is equal to approximately .62 miles.

Marsh: A wet area of land covered with grasses. The water in a marsh is often hidden by cattail, grasses, and other plants.

Maul: To attack and injure—either an animal or human being can be mauled.

Mph: An abbreviation for miles per hour, which is a unit of measurement for speed. One mile is equal to approximately 1.61 kilometers.

Pepper spray: A chemical used to repel bears and other dangerous creatures. It causes irritation and burning to the skin and eyes.

Poaching: The act of harvesting an animal at a time and place where it is illegal. Always follow the local hunting laws and regulations.

Process a kill: This is when an animal is butchered and cut up into pieces of meat to prepare for cooking. A kill can be processed by yourself or commercially.

Prey: Animals that are hunted for food—either by humans or other animals. It can also mean the act of hunting.

Roosting: What birds do when they rest upon a branch or a tree. Roosting keeps sleeping birds safe from predators.

Scout: To look ahead and observe an area. It is important to scout an area before hunting there. It helps you find evidence of your prey.

Suburbia: The area, people, and culture of a suburban, which is an area outside of a city or town where people live. It is often a small area full of houses.

Swamp: An area of wet land covered in grasses, trees, and other plant life. A swamp is not a good place to build a home, but it can be a good place to hunt.

Thicket: A collection of bushes and branches where small animals, like rabbits and rodents, like to hide.

Timid: A lack of confidence; shy. Rabbits, deer, and birds are often timid, which helps keep them alert and safe from predators.

Vegetation: All of the plant life in an area.

INDEX

FURTHER READING

Rezendes, Paul. *Tracking and the Art of Seeing: How to Read Animal Tracks and Sign.* Collins Reference; *2nd edition. 1999.*

Elbroch, Mark. *Mammal Track and Sign: A Guide to North American Species.* Stackpole Books. 2003.

Brown, Tom. *Tom Brown's Field Guide to Nature Observation and Tracking.* Berkley. 1986.

Lowery, James. *Tracker's Field Guide: A Comprehensive Manual for Animal Tracking.* Falcon Guides. 2013.

Cheney, Cleve. *The Comprehensive Guide to Tracking: In-Depth Information on How to Track Animals and Humans Alike.* Safari Press. 2013.

INTERNET RESOURCES

www.rabbithuntingonline.com
An excellent site for information on tracking and hunting rabbits.

www.naturetracking.com
A good site for beginners with lots of photos of animal and bird tracks and information on tracking schools.

www.deeranddeerhunting.com
This site contains plenty of information on tracking and hunting deer.

www.acornnaturalists.com
This website provides very good information on tracking animals and birds of North America and tracking schools.

ORGANIZATIONS TO CONTACT

The National Shooting Sports Foundation
Flintlock Ridge Office Center
11 Mile Hill Road
Newton, CT 06470-2359
Phone: (203) 426-1320
Fax: (203) 426-1087
Internet: https://www.nssf.org/

National Firearms Association
P.O. Box 49090
Edmonton, Alberta
Canada T6E 6H4
Phone: 1-877-818-0393
Fax: 780-439-4091
Internet: https://www.nfa.ca

The International Hunter Education Association
800 East 73rd Ave, Unit 2
Denver, CO 80229
Phone: 303-430-7233
Fax: 303-430-7236
Internet: https://www.ihea-usa.org

The National Wildlife Federation
11100 Wildlife Center Drive
Reston, VA 20190
Phone: 1-800-822-9919
Internet: https://www.nwf.org

PHOTO CREDITS

VIDEO CREDITS

Chapter 1
If that bare spot on your mantle is in need of a trophy buck, this video guide will get you on your way by helping you get the proper permits:
http://x-qr.net/1DmQ

Chapter 2
In this funny video, hunters break the rules and get caught by a game warden. A team of experienced hunters discusses with the warden why they think breaking these rules is unethical and unfair to other hunters:
http://x-qr.net/1Exj

Chapter 3
This video explains general hunting laws and regulations:
http://x-qr.net/1HmG

Chapter 4
This video gives a lot of practical advice for choosing a hunting spot on public land: http://x-qr.net/1EaB

AUTHOR'S BIOGRAPHY

Elizabeth Dee has hunted extensively in the southeast part of the United States for small and large game. She has also cleaned and cooked game for family meals. Elizabeth has been writing for over 25 years for magazines and web articles.